Animals in Their Habitats

Sea Animals

Francine Galko

Heinemann Library
Chicago, Illinois

Designed by Ginkgo Creative
Printed and bound in China

16 15 14
10 9

Library of Congress Cataloging-in-Publication Data
Galko, Francine.
   Sea animals / Francine Galko.
      p. cm. — (Animals in their habitats)
Includes bibliographical references (p.   ).
Summary: Explores the animals that make their habitat in the sea.
   ISBN 1-4034-0184-5 (HC), 1-4034-0441-0 (Pbk.)
   ISBN 978-1-4034-0184-7 (HC), 978-1-4034-0441-1 (Pbk.)
   1. Marine animals—Juvenile literature. 2. Ocean—Juvenile literature. [1. Marine animals.] I. Title.
   QL122.2 .G247 2002
   591.77—dc21

                     2001007660

Acknowledgments
The author and publishers are grateful to the following for permission to reproduce copyright material:
Cover photograph by www.brandoncole.com
p. 4 Nancy Simmermann/Bruce Coleman Inc.; p. 5 NASA/Visuals Unlimited; p. 6 Michael McCoy/Photo Researchers, Inc.; p. 7 Dr. Jeremy Burgess/Science Photo Library/Photo Researchers, Inc.; pp. 8, 11 P. Parks/OSF/Animals Animals; p. 9 Nick Caloyianis/National Geographic; p. 10 Scott Johnson/Animals Animals; p. 12 Carl Roessler/Animals Animals; p. 13 Tim Davis/Photo Researchers, Inc.; p. 14 HBOI/Visuals Unlimited; pp. 15, 29 Francois Gohier/Photo Researchers, Inc.; p. 16 Kim Reisenbechler/MBARI; p. 17 Ron Sefton/Bruce Coleman Inc.; p. 18 Andrew J. Martinez/Photo Researchers, Inc.; p. 19 P. Kay/OSF/Animals Animals; p. 20 Al Giddings/Al Giddings Images; p. 21 F. Gail/Visuals Unlimited; p. 22 Zig Leszczynski/Animals Animals; p. 23 James Watt/Animals Animals; p. 24 John Anderson/Animals Animals; p. 25 HBOI/Visuals Unlimited; p. 26 Fred Bavendam/Minden Pictures; p. 27 R. Kuiter/OSF/Animals Animals; p. 28 Tom Myers/Photo Researchers, Inc
Every effort has been made to contact copyright holders of any material reproduced in this book. Any omissions will be rectified in subsequent printings if notice is given to the publisher.

Some words are shown in bold, **like this.** You can find out what they mean by looking in the glossary.

To learn more about the dolphin on the cover, turn to page 13.

Contents

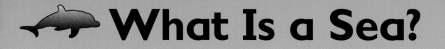 # What Is a Sea?

A sea is a kind of **habitat.** Seas are made of salty water. **Oceans** are large, open seas that go as far as you can see. All the seas on Earth are joined to one another.

Some seas have land all around them.
They have **channels** that connect them
to the ocean.

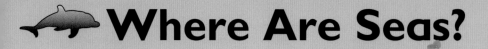 Where Are Seas?

Seas are all over the world. Every piece of land on Earth touches a sea in some way. There is more seawater on Earth than land.

Some seas are in warm parts of the world. People like to swim or walk on these **seashores.** Other seas are in very cold parts of the world. They sometimes have ice on them.

 Sea Homes

Animals live in different parts of the sea. A by-the-wind sailor floats in the sea like a tiny boat. Above the water, its body is filled with air. Under the water, its **tentacles** look for food.

These deep sea brittle stars do not like light. They often hide in the sand or under rocks in deep parts of the **ocean.**

Floating on the Water

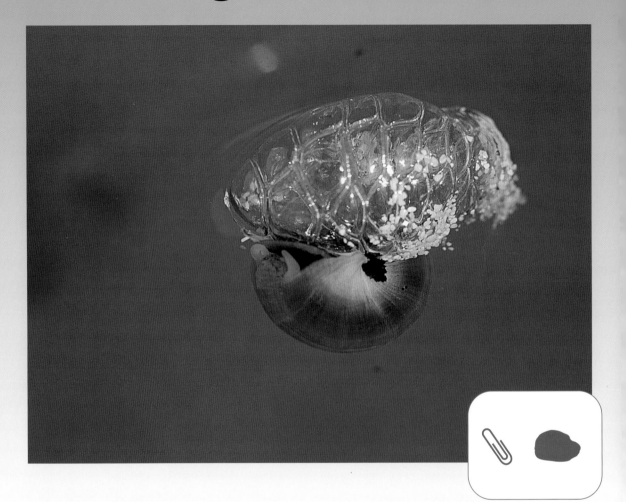

Some sea animals float on top of the water. The purple sea snail hangs from air bubbles on top of the water.

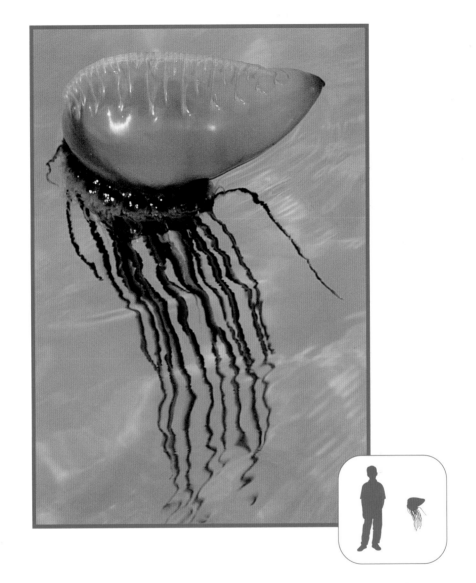

The Portuguese man-of-war has a purple
bag filled with air. The bag is like a balloon
that floats on top of the water. The wind
and **tide** move this animal across the water.

Living in Sunny Water

The water near the sea's **surface** gets lots of sunlight. Many plants grow in this part of the sea. Northern anchovy and other fishes live here.

Dolphins live here, too. Some dolphins live near the shore. Others live far out at sea. Dolphins swim like fish, but they aren't fish. They are **mammals** just like we are.

 # Living in Dim Water

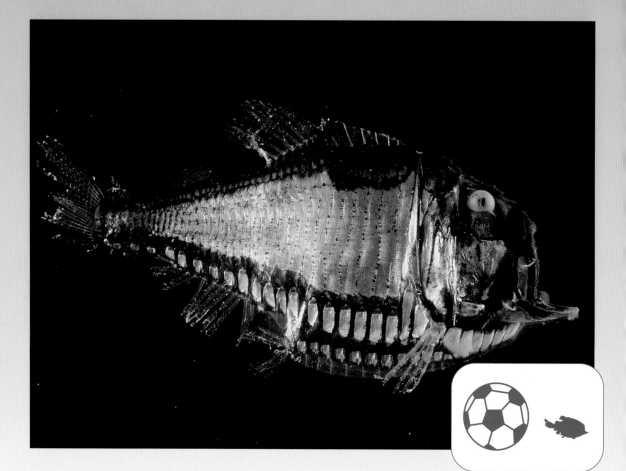

It's dim below the sunny water. Many animals here have **organs** that light up. The hatchet fish has light organs on its belly. **Prey** swim to the lights and the hatchet fish eats them.

Sperm whales sometimes dive into deeper water. When they come up from a dive, they blow wet air out of a **blowhole** in back of their heads.

Living in Dark Water

Large vampire squids live in very deep, dark water. They have large, blue eyes. Their arms have light **organs** and **spines**.

This red sea fan might look like a plant, but it's an animal. Its **tentacles** look like feathers. The tentacles help it catch tiny animals in the water.

Living on the Seafloor

Lobsters live on the **ocean** floor. As a lobster grows it **molts,** or sheds, its shell. It then grows a new shell.

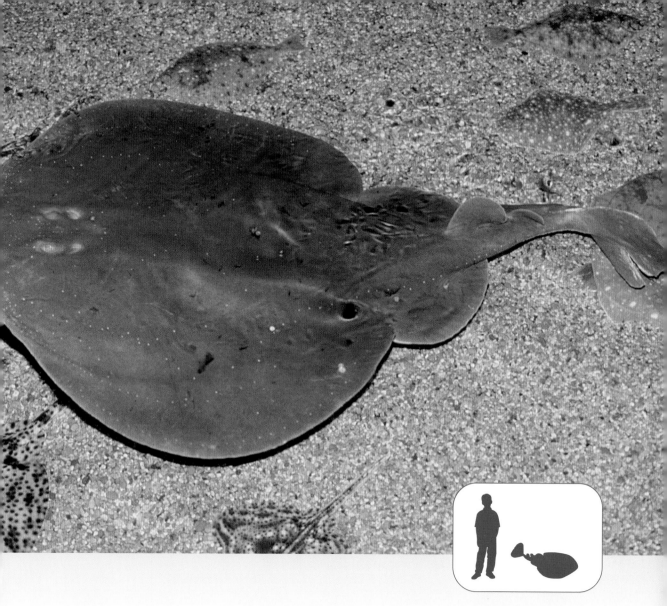

Electric rays are fishes with wide fins. They can give an electric **shock** that is strong enough to kill another fish. Then they eat the fish.

Living Near Deep Sea Vents

Deep sea vents look like chimneys on the **ocean** floor. Hot water and bubbles come out of the vents. It's hot enough to cook an animal, but giant tube worms like it here.

Giant white clams also live near deep sea vents. These clams and other animals are **adapted** to the heat and darkness.

 # Sea Predators

Some sea animals are **predators.** They hunt other animals. The football fish catches other fishes with a **spine** that acts like a fishing rod.

Great white sharks have strong teeth
that look like triangles. They hunt seals,
dolphins, and other sharks. Some will
even bite humans.

 # Hiding in the Sea

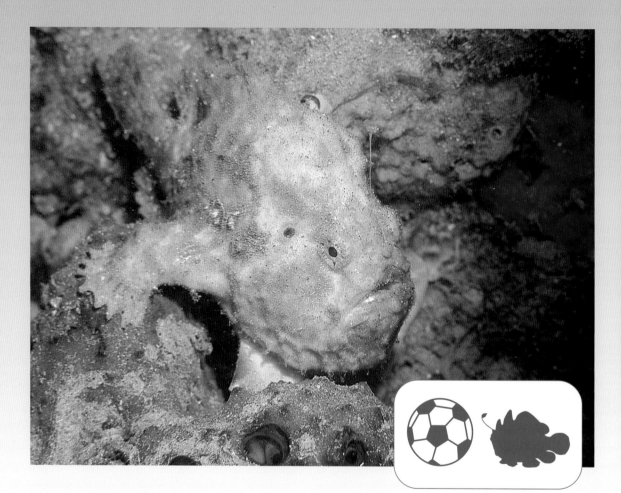

Frogfishes hide on the sea bottom. They have the same colors as the seafloor. Some frogfishes can change colors to hide better.

Lanternfishes are able to make their own light, just like fireflies. **Predators** cannot find them when they light up their tails. They don't know where to look.

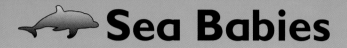 # Sea Babies

A female giant Pacific octopus lays many thousands of eggs in a rocky **den**. She stays with the eggs until they **hatch**. The baby octopuses then swim to the sea's **surface**.

A mother seahorse puts her eggs in a
pouch on the father's belly. Later, the
father gives birth to the baby seahorses.

Protecting Sea Animals

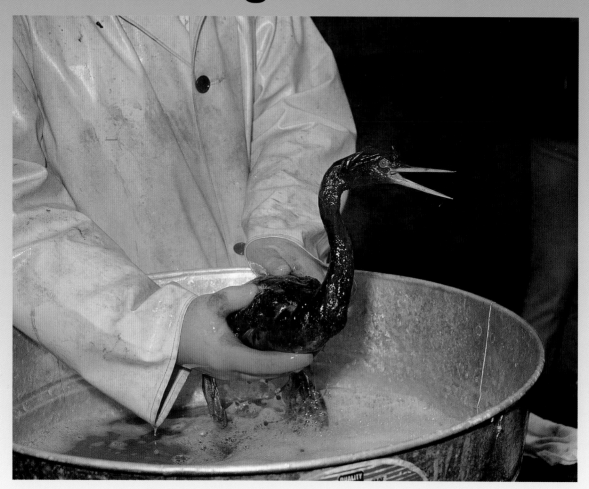

Sometimes people put garbage or **harmful chemicals** in the **ocean.** Oil that leaks from ships can hurt animals. Ships need strong sides so they won't break and leak oil.

Plastic bags, bottles, and the plastic rings that hold soda cans together kill a lot of sea animals. Don't leave these things at the **seashore** or throw them in the water.

 Glossary

adapt to fit into a place well

blowhole hole in the back of a whale's head that it breathes through

channel thin body of water that joins two larger bodies of water

den home underground or under rocks

habitat place where an animal lives

harmful chemical thing that can hurt plants and animals

hatch to come out of an egg

mammal animal, like humans, that has a backbone and hair or fur

molt to grow a new shell

ocean all the saltwater that covers Earth

organ part of the body, like the stomach, that carries out a job

pouch tiny bag on an animal's body

predator animal that hunts and eats other animals

prey animal that is hunted and eaten by another animal

seashore land near the sea

shock to hit suddenly with electricity

spine long, thin, stick-like part of an animal's body

surface top of the ocean

tentacle long, finger-shaped part of an animal's body that often catches food or stings prey

tide movement of water from the ocean onto the land twice each day

More Books to Read

Ashwell, Miranda and Andy Owen. *Seas and Oceans.*
  Chicago: Heinemann Library, 1998.

Robinson, Claire. *Dolphins.* Chicago: Heinemann Library, 1999.

Robinson, Claire. *Whales.* Chicago: Heinemann Library, 1999.

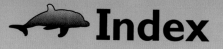# Index